SECRET LIFE OF A MOTHER

SECRET LIFE OF A MOTHER

BY HANNAH MOSCOVITCH
WITH MAEV BEATY AND ANN-MARIE KERR,
CO-CREATED WITH MARINDA DE BEER

PLAYWRIGHTS CANADA PRESS
TORONTO

For professional or amateur production rights, please contact:
Ian Arnold at Catalyst TCM
15 Old Primrose Lane, Toronto, ON M5A 4TI
416-568-8673 | ian@catalysttcm.com

LIBRARY AND ARCHIVES CANADA CATALOGUING IN PUBLICATION
Title: Secret life of a mother / by Hannah Moscovitch, with Maev Beaty and Ann-Marie Kerr.
Names: Moscovitch, Hannah, author. | Beaty, Maev, author. | Kerr, Ann-Marie, author.
Description: A play.
Identifiers: Canadiana (print) 2021032113X | Canadiana (ebook) 20210321156 | ISBN 9780369102836 (softcover) | ISBN 9780369102843 (PDF) | ISBN 9780369102850 (HTML)
Classification: LCC PS8626.O837 S43 2021 | DDC C812/.6—dc23

Playwrights Canada Press operates on land which is the ancestral home of the Anishinaabe Nations (Ojibwe / Chippewa, Odawa, Potawatomi, Algonquin, Saulteaux, Nipissing, and Mississauga), the Wendat, and the members of the Haudenosaunee Confederacy (Mohawk, Oneida, Onondaga, Cayuga, Seneca, and Tuscarora), as well as Metis and Inuit peoples. It always was and always will be Indigenous land.

We acknowledge the financial support of the Canada Council for the Arts, the Ontario Arts Council (OAC), Ontario Creates, and the Government of Canada for our publishing activities.

Canada Council for the Arts
Conseil des arts du Canada

ONTARIO ARTS COUNCIL
CONSEIL DES ARTS DE L'ONTARIO
an Ontario government agency
un organisme du gouvernement de l'Ontario

Canadä
ONTARIO CREATES | ONTARIO CRÉATIF

We dedicate this play to all mothers and those
who mother, including our own:
Mary Beaty,
Marilyn Kerr,
Meisie Oelofse de Beer,
and
Julie White

And to our children:
Anja and Frances,
Elijah,
Esmé,
and
Sophia

FOREWORD
MARINDA DE BEER

Marinda de Beer and Hannah Moscovitch. Photo by Dahlia Katz.

This play, this process, these women. After twenty-five years working as a stage manager, producer, and theatre collaborator, being a co-creator on *Secret Life of a Mother* was the single most important experience of my career. I was brought into the process after many years of drafts and research. Never have I been in a room where there was more vulnerability, honesty, trust, respect, and endless, terrifying creative risk-taking. This was a team of brilliant, strong, talented theatre warriors. Theatre royalty as far as I was concerned.

We spent endless hours writing grants. We aimed as high as we had ever aimed. What could we do if *we* were in charge

Hannah Moscovitch and Maev Beaty. Photo by Dahlia Katz.

of the process? Who would we hire to be our dream team? We budgeted to have our child care covered so that, for the first time in our careers, it wouldn't come out of our pay-cheques. We had performances offering free child care to patrons. We invited other brilliant women writers to come in and do preshow readings. We called all the shots, and we were so empowered I felt high each morning when I walked into the space.

This play was the biggest theatrical risk any of us ever took. Nothing is more exhilarating than being in charge of your own story. We wanted to bring the audience *inside* the experience of what it is to be a woman during this incredible life event. We knew we couldn't represent all women. But we could get as close as possible to representing our own truth. It was terrifying.

Marinda de Beer, Ann-Marie Kerr, and Maev Beaty. Photo by Dahlia Katz.

Hannah Moscovitch, the most prolific feminist playwright of her generation, always raw, honest, and presenting her audiences a new perspective on what they thought they already knew. This piece was different from anything she had already written; she would tell her own story. There were days when, suddenly, full of angst and passion, Hannah would yell out, "Guys! Don't you understand, this is MY VAGINA ON STAGE." And she was right. One of her closest and oldest friends, Maev Beaty, one of the most skilled, emotionally intelligent, talented actors in Canadian theatre, had the task of representing Hannah (and her vagina).

Maev had to *be* vulnerability. She was the perfect person for the task, as she was a master at vulnerability. But this time it was different. She had to be herself in a way she had never done before on stage. Not a character. The closer she

Hannah Moscovitch and Ann-Marie Kerr. Photo by Dahlia Katz.

could come to be fully herself, the greater the connection with the audience. As the stage manager, I had the privilege of bearing witness to the magic that occurred between Maev and the audience every night. The silences were fuller than I had ever felt. Each night was different. Each night was terrifying. Maev made room for the emotions of the audience in her performance. She looked out at them and saw them, felt them.

Ann-Marie Kerr, director, creator, actor, clown, wild, passionate, volatile, oozing enthusiasm and vulnerability had the task of steering the ship while we all had our hands on the wheel. Ann-Marie brought fireworks of creativity and curiosity to the room. When Maev and Hannah went too deeply into their intellect, Ann-Marie was the one to jolt the room back into the physical present. We trusted each

Ann-Marie Kerr, Marinda de Beer, and Maev Beaty. Photo by Dahlia Katz.

other enough to confront each other at every turn. We dug our heels in for the sake of truth. We laughed and cried and worried and fought. Mostly we flew. I held the room. I sat around the table while everyone confronted each other and then gently guided us back into the theatre to continue on the journey. We followed our deep, experienced intuition. We did our best not to worry about being liked, about being rewarded or valued, or at least to keep that part of ourselves in check.

The response blew us out of the water. We received hundreds of messages. The lobby was full of people after the show needing to talk about what just happened. I heard a twentysomething gentleman in the audience turn to his friend after the curtain call and say, "I need to call my mother." A woman who lost a son to suicide came back to see the show four times. We sold out. We were thrilled. But mostly we were humbled. We worked hard to get to where we are. We earned it. But, also, we allowed it to flow through us. It was a privilege. Thank you is an understatement.

Marinda de Beer has spent the last twenty-seven years stage managing in Toronto and across Canada. She has worked for Soulpepper, Canadian Stage, the Shaw Festival, Théâtre français de Toronto, Tarragon Theatre, and many other independent theatres. While stage managing, she was also a birth and post-partum doula for fifteen years, primarily serving the theatre community. She began producing in the last five years and is currently finishing her master's degree in Buddhism and Pastoral Studies.

Secret Life of a Mother was first produced by the SLOM Collective and the Theatre Centre from October 20 to November 11, 2018, at the Theatre Centre, Toronto, with the following cast and creative team:

Performer: Maev Beaty

Director: Ann-Marie Kerr
Producer and Stage Manager: Marinda de Beer
Scenic Design: Camellia Koo
Lighting Design: Leigh Ann Vardy
Associate Lighting Design: Kaileigh Krysztofiak
Projection: Cameron Davis
Sound Design: Debashis Sinha
Costume Design: Erika Connor
Props Builder: Haley Reap
Vocal Coach: Fides Krucker
Creative Producer for the Theatre Centre: Aislinn Rose

CHARACTERS

Hannah Moscovitch: Hannah is a writer: anti-expressive, anti-dramatic. Hannah is played by her real-life friend Maev Beaty.

On stage there are two aquariums full of water—one is small, the size of a fish tank you would see in a child's room, and one is large enough for a person to fit inside.

MAEV walks on and says hi to people. She holds a thin script in her hands.

MAEV: Hey, hi, I'm Maev Beaty, thanks for coming. *Secret Life of a Mother* is a play in five acts, so I hope you told your sitter midnight. Just kidding, it's only seventy minutes. Hannah . . . Moscovitch, who is a writer, wrote this . . . text . . . and then me and Ann-Marie Kerr, the director, and the whole team . . . have . . . been putting it up.

Beat.

So two months after Hannah gave birth to her son, Elijah, the mothering app she had on her phone sent her a tip: "Today, try getting back in the sack with your husband, even if you don't feel ready!"

Beat.

3

Exclamation mark.

Beat.

So a few years ago, Hannah and I set out to write about motherhood, because there wasn't a whole lot out there about it that was—or felt like it was—*for us*. We both have kids—Hannah has Elijah. He's four years old. I have Esmé. She's six. They're at home with their dads right now, because . . . well, I'm on stage playing . . . Hannah.

Beat.

MAEV *looks down at her thin script and reads from it:*

(*reading*) *Secret Life of a Mother* text notes. There is one character. The character is Hannah Moscovitch. Hannah is a writer: anti-expressive, anti-dramatic.

Beat.

You'll have to take my word for this: I'm poorly cast.

(*reading*) Hannah is played by her real-life friend Maev Beaty.

MAEV points to herself or raises her hand: "I am Maev."

And then Hannah says as her final text note: "So, guys, I've tried to record all of what happened: all the gross parts, the ones the blogs say are taboo."

Beat.

Act One . . . is titled Miscarriages. What a fun . . . title.

MAEV walks over to the aquarium.

The lights go dark. A low rumble is heard.

MAEV PERFORMING HANNAH: In December 2015 I was fourteen weeks pregnant, and I went to the IWK and had an ultrasound of the baby.

MAEV slips a piece of paper from the script she's holding into the small fish tank, and a video of Elijah

*appears. In the video—which is a close-up—Elijah is
in a bathtub. He's two years old and he's laughing and
talking, though the video is mute.*

My organs, and then, between them, a small fetus, moving, in
spasms. There was so much movement that the doctor made
a joke about how my fetus was going to win the Stanley Cup.

The video of Elijah turns to static.

A few days later I woke up, in the afternoon, and turned
over, and . . . something *sloshed*. I stood up and . . . cupped
my hands between my legs, and they filled up with blood.
Christian, my husband, was watching hockey down-
stairs, and he came running up and by then there was a

lot of blood on the floor around me—a pool of blood is actually . . .

Beat.

I was standing in a pool of blood.

Beat.

My hands were shaking, but my thoughts stayed calm, which might describe . . . shock . . . ? Christian was having trouble putting sentences together. I remember thinking, "Okay, well, I guess I'm miscarrying again."

"Yeah." Yep.

Yeah.

In emergency—this was right before Christmas, so doctors' offices were closed and the QEII emerg in Halifax was packed with seventy or so people—there was, no joke, a guy who looked like he'd taken an axe to the forehead and the nurses had given him a little plastic receptacle to bleed into, and he was, you know, sitting in the waiting room waiting his turn—and I told the triage desk what was happening and how many weeks along I was and—this was great but weird—they got me a wheelchair and took me straight in.

My first miscarriage, I'd sat in emergency for three hours. This time, I waited less than a minute.

In the wheelchair I asked the nurse what—why . . . ? She said, "Well, you're fourteen weeks along . . . Most miscarriages happen between seven to nine weeks . . . " So, yeah, the nurse thought I was probably going to have a—I might have a . . . more difficult miscarriage.

I was taken into a room and then a doctor wheeled in a portable ultrasound machine. He held the paddles against my stomach, which was a little distended—my stomach was distended because I'd started to show—and there were four or five residents and nurses in the room by then and they were all *very focused* on the screen. I looked over at Christian because . . . he kept trying to take a sip from a coffee that he'd finished hours ago—or, no, actually the coffee was miscarriage number one because of course this time he didn't have time to get a coffee—and, on the screen, there's the baby, hanging suspended, and not moving.

> MAEV *looks down at the paper in the aquarium. Static plays on it. Elijah flickers up on the screen for a few seconds, and then the static comes back.*

The doctor started pushing down harder on my stomach with the paddles to try and get the baby to move. It was . . . weirdly silent in the room: the medical staff were all glued to the screen. I remember how—yeah—*weird* it was to see residents and nurses this emotionally involved.

The baby still hadn't moved.

*MAEV looks down at the static again. Elijah flickers
up on the screen for a few seconds, and then Elijah is
gone and the static comes back.*

The doctor started speaking to the monitor. He said,
"Come on, little guy, come on, move."

*The lights shift. MAEV drops out of playing HANNAH
and speaks directly to an audience member.*

MAEV: Hey, hi, this is Maev—Hannah writes here that the
doctor was talking to her baby, so can you say "come on,
little guy, move." Can you say that so we can hear what it
sounds like to hear that, with a voice that's not mine. So
your uh . . . voice?

(to the audience at large) And I promise I won't do this the
whole show.

They say it:

AUDIENCE MEMBER: Come on, little guy, move.

MAEV: Are you a doctor? You are very good at this. You're
hired. Can you say it four more times, with a few seconds'
pause between each time? And can you say it softly, but
also loud enough for the whole audience to hear, like you're
coaxing a . . . fetus.

They say it:

AUDIENCE MEMBER: Come on, little guy, move. Come on, little guy, move. Come on, little guy, move. Come on, little guy, move.

As they speak, MAEV switches back to playing HANNAH, responding emotionally to the words as HANNAH would—trying to stay pragmatic, trying not to cry. The audience and HANNAH listen to the audience member until:

MAEV PERFORMING HANNAH: And the baby . . . *moves.* He moves!!!

The video of Elijah reappears in the tank on the piece of script—Elijah is laughing in the bathtub.

His hand. Then his body contracts.

Beat.

And uh . . . the room goes crazy. The doctor shakes Christian's hand.

MAEV makes a face. The doctor shaking Christian's hand strikes her as offside, sexist.

And one of the residents says to me, "I needed some good news!"

MAEV takes the paper out of the aquarium and puts the dripping sheet onto the back of her script. The image of Elijah is gone.

Yeah and the uh . . .

The whole time Elijah was . . . not moving—I was thinking . . .

"It's okay. I won't be a mother: that's okay. I probably . . . wasn't going to be very good at it anyway."

Beat.

The lights shift.

A year and a half earlier, in June 2014, I was by myself in New York City on a work trip, for one day, twenty-four hours. I was eleven weeks pregnant and not telling anyone, and I was nauseated, and I kept being surprised that no one was noticing—or at least not commenting on—*how many* meal-replacement beverages I was drinking.

I went back to my hotel room and knelt over the toilet and couldn't vomit, and then I made myself get up and get into the bed. Then I had a nightmare. I was in an ambulance, and then a doctor leaned over my hospital bed and said, "I'm sorry, you've had a miscarriage."

Then I woke up.

I was in a Holiday Inn, Lower East Side.

I went into the bathroom to pee. I pulled my sweatpants down and . . .

> MAEV *walks over the tank, which is lowlit with brown murky lights.*

There was uh . . . brown blood on my underwear.

I uh . . . sat there, for a while, looking down at it . . .

I went and got my laptop—

> *The murky lights snap to a blue screen glow.*

—and sat on the toilet with it and googled "blood during pregnancy eleven weeks." I got a lot of sites that said spotting is normal at eleven weeks and probably it's nothing, which is surprising because usually when I diagnose myself using Google I end up convinced I have Crohn's disease. And autism.

Maybe I didn't click on the links that I should have, because I wanted to think I was fine because I was in New York City, and I didn't want to have to find a hospital or work out how to get the travel insurance off my credit card. Also, I was about to fly home to Halifax, then onto Budapest,

Hungary, to work on a TV show, and I didn't want that to get fucked up.

And I wanted the baby.

The lights shift to suggest the terminal at Newark.

Next morning I was in the terminal at Newark Airport waiting to board my flight home, and I was walking around trying to find a place to plug my laptop in, and the airport was packed, there were no available plugs, and no seats, and fast food trash on the floor, like just mashed into the floor, and I was thinking to myself, "This is a shitty terminal. I hate Newark!," and I went into the washroom, which I was avoiding doing . . .

The lights shift back to the low brown lights from the hotel bathroom.

There was more blood on my underwear.

And I had this eerie thought: my nausea's better.

The lights shift to suggest an airplane.

On the flight home I kept thinking through what I would say if I had to go up to a flight attendant: "Hey, I'm miscarrying. Should I do that in my seat, or should I go into the bathroom and miscarry in the bathroom? Where on this airplane do I miscarry?"

The lights shift to suggest a hospital.

By the time I got to Halifax the blood was . . . fresh blood. Me and Christian went to emergency and sat in the waiting room and then various triage rooms for three hours and told jokes and watched shitty talk show TV on silent, and had coffees and bags of chips from the vending machines, and scrolled through our Twitter feeds, and then a doctor came into our room and said, "Do you know what a miscarriage is, because there's no pregnancy hormone in your blood."

Then I said this weird thing, I said, "Oh yeah, I know what they are: my friend had one a few years ago." And yeah—I don't know why I told the doctor that detail about my friend? I don't often . . . talk much unless . . . ? But my friend's miscarriage stuck with me, maybe that's why . . . ?

The lights shift. MAEV drops out of the character of HANNAH and adlibs.

MAEV: Hi, it's Maev again . . . I want to admit to you that I am the friend that Hannah thought of during her miscarriage. I had described my miscarriage to her—I'd actually described a whole lot about my miscarriage to her. Uhm, I told her for example about the hemorrhaging that happened a week after the event, which I did not know was going to happen. And I was uh at my accountant's office—artbooks.to, they're amazing, I recommend them—and I—I had to go into the bathroom at the uh accountant's office, and I was sitting there in the—the bathroom, like on a toilet full of blood, and I thought, "This is an amazing metaphor for taxes."

I had also told her about the nurses that tended to me in the hospital at emergency the night of the uh miscarriage itself. And I think these . . . nurses were like eleven or twelve years old? They, uh—they made such a—an amazing mess of taking my blood—like there was blood just like everywhere—and one of them literally said to the other at one point, "I am soooooo bad at this!" Which made my husband laugh and uh . . . homicidal.

But the thing that I . . . I told Hannah about my miscarriage, which I did not even realize until I said it to Hannah, was that the feeling of sadness when the doctor said, "I'm sorry, there is no heartbeat," was so simple and uncomplicated, unlike almost all the other sadnesses that I can think of in life, like about work or whatever. The feeling was so pure . . . that it was almost sweet. I wanted to tell you that. And now I'm going to go back in, to Hannah.

MAEV touches the script to indicate she's performing
HANNAH again. The lights shift to suggest a doctor's
office.

MAEV PERFORMING HANNAH: So the material from the miscarriage was still uh . . . In me.
The next day, my family doctor looked at the notes from the ER, and the material was a little bigger than they like for pharmaceutical methods, and so she told us we should

be hustling over to the IWK at seven a.m. the next morning, bright and early, because they do all their D&C surgeries on Thursdays, and maybe they'd be able to squeeze me into the operating room slate if I went over and asked very nicely

And I

I'd been up most of the night in the ER and

The baby was gone and

I had work deadlines and I was

I know I sounded weary or maybe even hostile when I said "What if I don't do that?"

"What if I don't 'hustle' anywhere?"

> *The lights shift to suggest the darkness of coming around from anaesthetic and an operating room. Abstracted operating room sounds are heard.*

At the IWK, the next morning, bright and early—the surgical team was talking about me while I was still coming around from the anesthetic.

They said, "Her cervical clamp is still in."

And, "Ask her why she's crying."

I opened my eyes and there was a nurse looking down at me and she said, "Are you in pain?"

> *Beat.*

> HANNAH *cries.*

> *Beat.*

I wasn't in uh
The pain was fine
I didn't know why I was crying.
It was a weird . . . !
A doctor came over and said, "Miscarriages are routine,"
and, "It's okay, most women go on to carry to term."
And I said "yeah" and I
Knew he was right!

In the bed across from me, another woman who has also just
had the same procedure, she was crying too. The nurses said
it was because her husband couldn't get the day off work.

The lights shift to suggest an airplane.

A few days after the miscarriage, I was on another flight,
this time to Budapest, to go and work on the TV show, and
I was working on an episode of the TV show that I'd fallen
behind on, so I was trying to catch up so I could do a good
job, but halfway through the flight . . . !

I *really* thought I'd managed to avoid having a miscarriage
on a fucking airplane, turns out . . . ! I had nothing with
me, stupidly. I stuffed handfuls of that cheap airplane toilet
paper into the crotch of my pants, and then sat on a fucking
mound of bloody toilet paper. But even still I stained the
fuck out of my seat with . . . "miscarriage," or, I didn't even
know what the fuck was wrong with me—if it was more
miscarrying or a hemorrhage or what the fuck—and I was
starting to think that when we landed I was going to have

to find a fucking Hungarian hospital, and get my goddamn fucking travel insurance off my credit card, but the main thing I was thinking was "I don't have fucking time for this."

MAEV reaches her hand between her legs and pulls out pieces of bloody tissue—miscarriage. She holds her hand out to the audience.

MAEV goes and, as the small tank lights up, puts her hand into the tank. We see the bloody pieces of tissue float through the water to the bottom of the tank.

The below section is a recording of HANNAH speaking. As the recording plays, MAEV washes the rest of the bloody chunks off her hands in the small fish tank and cleans up the floor. Then she holds up a piece of paper from her script, onto which the pre-recorded video is projected.

HANNAH: *(from video)* Before I had Elijah, I thought about myself as a mother.
Here are some things I thought I'd be bad at.

Uh, like—and this will take some explaining—I don't spend a lot of time in the physical world.
I'm in my mind a lot of the time.
Uh, often it's at insensitive times, when people are talking to me
Uh, in high school I developed an ability to not listen
I think it's the only thing I learned to do in high school
But it often isn't deliberate, I just tune out

There's a phrase in psychology for this, it's "being a dick."
Just kidding.
No, it's "domestic deafness."

I do it at dangerous times, like when I'm crossing the street
(uh, I've had four car accidents—two as a pedestrian). I just
walked out into the street.

Uh, one time, when I was in theatre school training to be
an actor, I was standing backstage, and I tuned out, and I
didn't go on stage. My classmates were forced to improvise.
And the play was *Henry VI* by Shakespeare.

The improv sounded like this:
"Quoth! Dost thou wonder where Queen Margaret be?"

It's like there's a video game playing in my head all the time
And I play it to the exclusion of everything else, in particular the physical world, the world that I assumed babies
inhabited.

> *The video ends.* MAEV *puts the piece of paper she was
> holding—onto which the video was projected—back
> into her script.* MAEV *addresses the audience as herself:*

MAEV: So, we asked that Hannah record that part of the text
about why Hannah was going to be a bad mother, because
it's so particular to her. But uh when I rewatched, this I
didn't one hundred per cent get why it was going to make
her a bad mother. So I asked her, and this is what she said:

An audio recording of HANNAH *plays:*

HANNAH: (*from audio*) Aside from being scared I would tune out, and Elijah would fall out a window, I was also scared about how long I can go without speaking. I had a bad feeling I wouldn't talk to Elijah enough, and his language skills . . . wouldn't develop.

The lights shift.

MAEV: Act Two, Labour. *Yeah!* Straight down the birth canal of this . . . show.

Beat.

MAEV PERFORMING HANNAH: When Maev and I started working on this project, we had an intern who was twenty-five years old, and she was in the room when Maev told her birth story, and later the intern whispered to me, "That was horrifying."

MAEV drops out of playing HANNAH *and adlibs about what was horrifying about her birth story. She goes and gets her laptop from under a chair in the audience and uses it to show pictures of her body post-birth.*

MAEV: So I think I know why she said that—hi, it's Maev again. So my labour actually went pretty well—for uh uh quite a long time for . . . several hours—uh, until I got to the pushing part. So, when we got to the pushing part, I pushed

so hard that I gave myself two black eyes, which I did not know was a thing. And also I um burst the blood vessels in the whites of my eyes and I gave myself a mask of uh burst blood vessels from my hairline down to my breasts.

MAEV holds up the laptop displaying the photos of her face and shows them to the audience.

So, um, here's some pictures . . . here we go . . .

MAEV scrolls.

So can everyone see that?

Can you see that at the back, uh . . . ?

MAEV zooms in.

So this is—this is a week and a half after. So this is me looking quite a bit better. And uh . . . yeah: so you know those pictures of like smiling new moms holding their newborns? So mine are all like *Twin Peaks* . . . really scary . . .

So not only that, but the day after uh the birth, I asked the nurse—she came into the hospital room—and I was like, "Can you check me out down there?" And she looked, and she said, "Oh yeah you've given yourself, um, rug burn on your ass cheeks from pushing against the table so hard." (But she didn't say ass cheeks because she's a nurse. I don't remember what she said—what term . . . but anyways . . .)

MAEV shows the photograph of her rug-burned ass and zooms in on it.

Yeah, there we go, that's them. So can everyone see that. Uh, so that's a weeping sore there. And that's a yeah . . . And my husband's over there: hi, Alan!

MAEV closes the laptop.

So the reason I think that uh this happened—that this damage happened—was because at one point uh they asked me to lie on my back, and the contractions slowed down a little bit, and I thought that I was maybe doing it wrong, maybe I was, uh—uh, boring. So I started pushing when I wasn't really . . . So basically what happened was I was *performing* pushing.

So I think that's why the intern said "that was horrifying." Yeah . . . Now back to Hannah.

MAEV puts her laptop away and goes back to performing HANNAH.

MAEV PERFORMING HANNAH: There's a version of birth on TV and in movies that we're familiar with. It's how sex used to be shown. A kiss, then a kiss with some tongue, and then a pan up to a tree in blossom.

Labour is usually a montage sequence: the woman pushes, her face is sweaty, and then there's a baby in her arms and she's looking worn out but fulfilled. The sheets are blue or white. And the baby is usually between one and three months old. I know this because I work in TV and so I know a little about what babies are available to be cast.

I'd been trying to finish an episode of a TV show I was writing before the baby came, so I'd gone to bed at two a.m.

When I woke up around four a.m., the pain felt a lot like what I'd been feeling the last few day—pressure on my cervix. So I went into the spare room and watched Netflix. I was halfway through an episode of *The Good Wife* when the pain got bad, and I . . .

Kept watching the episode! As in what's going to happen with Alicia and her husband, who fucks hookers but is nice to her now, and will she win in court this week? And then at some point the pain was so bad I couldn't lay still, and I finally clued in that I was nine months pregnant, five days past my due date. I've heard of this happening before: a woman I know googled "forty weeks pregnant water coming out of vagina."

So the first thing I did was . . .

I wrote an email to my bosses, the showrunners, so that I could send them the episode of TV I was working on. Then I opened the episode doc, and I edited it for a while, uh . . . yeah, while I was having contractions.

Yeah. Yep.

Then I woke up Christian.

Christian's response was, "I'm too tired for it to be happening." Which was him being funny.

But he did go back to sleep and I did lay beside him in pretty bad pain for a while being polite about it.

Ahead of my labour, Christian and Amy, my doula, asked me what I was scared of. I wasn't scared of labour pain being *bad* (because I'd been in a car accident that knocked out six of my front teeth and then I spent a couple of years having surgeries to reconstruct them, and, also, *I was hit by a car*, and *that hurt*) but I was afraid of what the pain would make me *do*. I was scared of what was at the bottom of my psyche that I might let go of when the pain was bad, that it would shortcut me to my true self, and I'd find out I was actually a . . . bad person.

For the first twelve hours the pain was fine, or, *not fine*, but . . . I was in my bathtub and my water broke and the amniotic fluid moved with so much velocity that I could see it pumping out of me *through* the bathwater. And now it was like someone was punching down onto my cervix, and it was stinging as though things in there had started to rip, and that's when I started wanting to push.

In the cab on the way to the hospital, I could tell that the cab driver was worried about his seats, so I tried to hold in my amniotic fluid. When we got out of the cab I was heaving and I could see people looking at me the way you look at a person who's in the middle of a physical crisis.

In reception, the nurses were freaked out when they saw me. I was saying "*I want to push!*" So they started asking emergency questions, like my blood type, and "do you think you're going to deliver in this elevator?"

Upstairs, on the maternity ward, the nurse examined me, and . . .

> *MAEV PERFORMING HANNAH plunges her arm into the fish tank. Onto her palm is projected a video of Esmé as a baby.*

. . . no.
I'm trying to, uh
They're talking and I'm uh trying to
Cooperate and
The nurse's saying the baby's way down my birth canal putting pressure on my cervix and that's why I want to push so badly

25

And Christian's looking at them and nodding
And someone somewhere's screaming . . . ?
But they're saying
I'm only three centimetres dilated and "good job" on those
three centimeters but
I have to be ten centimetres before I start to push so at
least another four or five hours and maybe more if I keep
pushing down because . . . I'm going to rip the shit out of
my cervix
And Christian says, "But it's been twelve hours . . . "
And no, they say, I can't push.
And Christian's nodding yeah.

And then I start barfing
And there are *no contractions*
What the fuck is fucking "contractions"—it's just one long
fucking contraction!
And the whole time
The *only thing* I want is to do is push
And all that went on for the next four or five hours!
And for those hours, the nurses and Christian and my
doula say to me every few seconds, "Don't push."

MAEV steps out of her role as HANNAH and goes up to
the audience and says:

MAEV: Hey, so we get a sense of this, can you four people
say "don't push" over and over again for the next . . . five
hours. Just kidding, I'm just kidding.

MAEV goes back to playing HANNAH. Beat.

MAEV PERFORMING HANNAH: And here's where I learn
what's at the bottom of my psyche: turns out I'm very sorry.
I said sorry over and over again
For vomiting so many times
For getting blood on the floor
For screaming
For not being able to handle it, handle the pain.

MAEV plunges her hand back in the water.

And oh no
Oh god
I'm fucked
And at the end of the five hours
They examine me again and
I'm four centimetres dilated—*only one more centimetre
because I'm swelling my cervix shut*
My doctor and the nurses
They're saying I need medication . . .
Which . . . !
That's fine!
They hand me the tube to breathe in the gas, and I scream
into it
And they have to tell me
"Stop screaming *down* the tube, breathe the gas *in*."

And then there's bright lights and colours and I have this
thought, which is, "Who's screaming?"

And then the nurses are prying the tube out of my hands
and I've hit the limit of the amount of gas I can have
I hear them saying it's been twenty-four hours . . .
They're worried my . . . m . . . muscles will start to
. . . seize . . .
And it's four a.m. again and . . .
Christian's . . .
And . . . the pain is . . .
And I don't . . .
The pain's like . . . a hole I'm in . . .
But even then, even then . . . I know I have to . . .
I have to . . .
Because I know this isn't even . . .

I know that what's to come, the baby . . .
. . . is the hard part.

> *MAEV walks toward the big fish tank. She once again catches a projected video of HANNAH on a page from her manuscript.*

HANNAH ON VIDEO: Here's the other thing I thought I'd be bad at as a mother: I thought I'd have a hard time . . . stopping work . . .

. . . Because I'm a workaholic, which . . .

. . . Is weirdly socially acceptable, as though, what I'm saying is, *"I'm amazing,"* or, *"Watch out for me, I'm ambitious!"* But in my case, I'm *not*. I'm saying I don't feel safe unless I'm working because . . . I don't know . . . because . . . my family's like that . . . because . . . I'm Jewish, and I come from a long line of people who don't feel safe, because our neighbours regularly got it into their heads that if they killed us all it would solve everything, culminating in Nazis. So—yeah—for whatever reason I am a workhaholic and I was worried that if I kept working at the same rate after I gave birth, I'd burn out or . . . worse. Or what would happen?

> *MAEV undresses and climbs up to stand on the large-sized aquarium's platform.*

MAEV: Act Three: Birth.

MAEV PERFORMING HANNAH: I got an epidural and, at the twenty-seven-and-a-half hour mark, I'm finally allowed to push.

The nurses ask me if I want to see, and I say, "*Yeah!*" So they wheel in a mirror, and in the mirror I see a painting by Gustave Courbet from 1866. I saw it in the Musee D'Orsay in Paris. It's a closeup view of the genitals and abdomen of a naked woman, lying on a bed with her legs spread. The painting is called *Origins of the World*.

The doctor points to a tuft of hair—it's the top of Elijah's head—that I can see in my pubic hair!

MAEV climbs into the tank. She goes into the fetal position.

When Elijah comes out, he looks at me, very alert.

Beat.

I'm wheeled onto the recovery ward, and . . .
I'm holding Elijah and he was crying, and I asked the nurses, "Oh no, why's he crying?" And the nurse says newborns are scared because they were in the womb and now . . .
They're on a fucking hospital ward. I say to Elijah
I say

MAEV *holds her script between her arms in the aquar-*
ium and the video projection of Elijah, at two years
old, laughing and talking in the bath (but muted)
flicks up on her script.

"It's okay, it's okay, it's . . . okay. I'm . . . I'm your . . . mother
. . . it's okay." . . .
I sat up with him, ice packs between my legs, and rocked him . . .
Pieces of Hebrew prayers came back to me . . . from syna-
gogue or . . . seders or . . . ?
As though my father was singing or . . .

(singing) Shm'a Israel Adonai Elochainu Adonai Echad . . .
Baruch shem k'vod malchoutanu, l'olam va'ed.

Also Celine Dion.

From my hospital bed, I sent a photo of Elijah to my father. He wrote back: "This photo reminds me of you. You had that same alert look when you were born. He's your son."

MAEV gets out of the tank.

Four days after Elijah is born, Christian is with him in the spare room
He was trying to give me a chance to sleep a little
The pain was bad.
I couldn't find a good position.
I got a mirror out
I looked between my legs and I saw the hole, the normal hole that is the entrance to my vagina, and then inside the hole there was a second *massive gaping hole* as though the whole side of my vagina had opened up

MAEV disappears into the darkness at the back of the stage.

I ran out of the room and found my husband and I said: "I think I need my mother to come here."

And he said, "What about my mother?"

And I said "IIIIIIIIIIIIIII NEEEEEEEEEEEED MYYYYYYYY MOTTTHHHHHEEEEEEERRRRRRRRRRR."

MAEV climbs up to sit on the aquarium's platform.

At my doctor's office, my doctor examined me and she said, "Your stitches pulled out so the side of your vagina has opened up."

She drew a picture of it for me.

> *MAEV puts a piece of paper in the water then picks it up and tears it open.*

The whole side of my vagina had opened up and was now nothing.

> *MAEV affixes the piece of paper to the side of the aquarium. Photos of HANNAH's happy family are projected on it. Meanwhile, MAEV goes and sits down stage on a chair.*

MAEV: Act Four. Bad Mother.

> *During the below section, MAEV PERFORMING HANNAH sits close to the audience and remains very still:*

MAEV PERFORMING HANNAH: I lay Elijah in the middle of our bed. I go over to the closet and I put away some underwear. I'm unpacking our suitcases after a trip to Montreal. I'm still standing by the closet, tuned out, thinking about work, I don't know for how long. I hear Elijah moving. I turn around and I see him slide down the side of the bed headfirst, catch for a moment on the frame, and then hit the floor. He's only three months old.

Photo by Kyle Purcell.

I'm in Banff, working, and I let Elijah play in the sink. He fits right in it and seems happy. I have a feeling this is a bad idea, but I let him do it anyway because we're in a hotel room in winter and there's so little for a baby to do. While he's playing in the sink, I lose focus. I think about other things. I hear him scream. I look down and he's turned on the hot water tap.

Elijah and I are in the airport by ourselves. Christian is meeting us at home in Halifax with a station wagon load of our crap. I've opened a new play, then gone straight into a TV room for a week, then packed all our stuff up into the station wagon late into the night, and of course Elijah is still waking up two times a night for milk and I've only had three hours of sleep. Elijah cries and throws

himself on the ground at the gate because he can't understand that we have to wait to get on the flight and I carry
him into the disabled-slash-family bathroom and I lock
the door. I sit against the wall in the public bathroom and
I watch Elijah unroll all the toilet paper. I call Christian. I
tell him I am too tired to get on the flight with a baby by
myself: I don't know if I can get on the flight. I say coffee
doesn't work anymore. I say I am so tired I don't know
what will happen on this flight, that I feel like I don't even
like Elijah right now, that I feel physically angry at him
like I want to hit him. I say all of this while Elijah is putting his hands into something wet on the floor that might
either be spilled air freshener or urine.

Beat.

And yeah—yeah, awesome.

Beat.

Yeah.

Pause.

I—yeah—feel . . . not good about . . . myself.

Beat.

And even if Maev plays me I'll still be exposed.

Beat.

It's the taboo shit, which is . . . yeah, and my ripped vagina and it's . . . my feelings, which I don't like to . . . And then the worst is . . . me as a . . .

Pause.

Listen, I can work on myself, as a mother, but I feel fucked.

Beat.

I feel—yeah—fucked—either way, because . . .

Beat.

Banff only had standardized rooms, and they didn't have cribs or any facilities, and I said yes to that gig, and that's my workaholism, but I do have to take some gigs, and I let Elijah play in the sink because when I took him into the corridor and he made high-pitched sounds, I got hostile looks, and I know as a mother I have to hold my ground and if people are shitty about him being a baby, that's their problem, but holy fuck, between taking Elijah on an airplane and having to eat in restaurants with him, because there's no kitchen in my hotel room, I'm facing a lot of hostility. And he's waking up at twelve a.m. and two a.m. and four a.m. for milk, and then I'm working all day as though I don't have a baby, and then I am tuning out because I do that but also because on this little sleep it's pretty hard to stay with it.

Beat.

And—yeah—this whole mothering thing is such a racket, like, "Hey, be a mother, that's super, just as long as you don't expect us to set up any shit that would make being a mother feasible, and also, if you aren't able to be a good mother in these fucked-up circumstances, well hey, fuck you."

Beat.

And it's funny: I'm a TV writer, and I've mostly written mothers as . . . villains.

Beat.

Act Five. My Friend, Maev.

Beat.

Maev would come over, sometimes, in the long summer we had together when Elijah was one and Esmé was three, at the Stratford Festival, working on a play together. And we'd be coming off of our different shit—Maev would've spent eleven hours in the ER with Esmé, who had diarrhea, trying to get her to drink Pedialyte while working to get her lines down, and I'd be being a mom and in rehearsal, jogging home on lunch breaks to nurse Elijah and making elaborate snacks for the nanny, as if to say, with my elaborate snacks, "Please fucking eat this snack so you can look after Elijah." Maev and I would drink, and that meant a lot to me, not because we said meaningful things but because . . .

Beat.

I'd admit to her that, say, when I was with Elijah, I went and hid along a forest trail so I could nurse him without getting my tits out in public, but it turned out it wasn't a forest trail at all, it was the path from the parking lot to the theatre, and then whole busloads of fucking tourists traipsed by me and I was like . . . "Hey, so these are my tits, come see my show, it's gonna be *great. Enjoy your matinee!*"

Beat.

We'd talk about, you know, whatever was funny and terrible and happening.

Beat.

And yeah, at some point Maev said to me, "Mothers make lives but they also make deaths," and that . . . ! Stuck with me. And I admitted to Maev that I couldn't stop thinking about it, because I was the one there picking Elijah up and holding him when he fell over, or when he was scared, and . . . I wasn't going to be there for Elijah's death—I mean hopefully!—and he'd die without me . . . there to . . . hold him, and it could be a bad death, he could be alone, and I . . . was . . . picturing it, and . . . I didn't want it to happen that way, and what could I do about it? And Maev said, "Help him to know how to love people, so when he's dying, someone's there."

Beat. MAEV steps out of performing HANNAH.

MAEV: Hi it's Maev again. I really want to tell you what I remember about that summer with uh Hannah.

The previous summer the Stratford Festival had um offered me a three-show contract, which was thrilling, it was like a dream come true for me, and I—like my face was on two posters. And uh it was uh really exciting, but it did also mean that we were going to have to live in separate cities again . . . the family, and it was going to be hard on Alan to be apart from Esmé, and I was going to have to rely on my parents a lot. And then a couple of the shows were very popular and so they kept adding performances, and so I was working up to seventy-five hours a week, and I was still nursing Esmé, and there were a lot of late nights and early mornings, and uh by the middle of the season I was fucked. I was drinking and I was smoking, and I was having a lot of dark thoughts. And I felt that I was failing in every direction: as a mother, as an artist, as a wife, as a daughter. And I felt so much guilt and shame for wanting to take that gig, for wanting to work, and I told my friend Hannah this. And she said, "But it's who you are. It's who you are: you are the mother and you are the artist. It's not a choice outside of yourself that you're making. And who you are is who are: you are an art monster, and you do not have to be ashamed." And when she said that to me, she set me free.

Okay . . . ! So . . .

Beat.

So Hannah wrote a text note here. It says, "Hey, this is weird but, guys, I have this picture in my mind of Maev floating or flying, so I'm writing it in here, just, you know, I don't know, weird."

MAEV tries to get up on the chair and float for a second, then gives up on it. She goes off stage. Behind the black curtains, we hear sounds:

Uh, fuck. Uh.

A ladder clangs.

The curtain opens and MAEV is flying.

We discover that there has been aerial circus silks hanging up stage of the curtain and plexiglass wall the whole time. MAEV transforms from a flying woman with wings to the shape of a curled baby in utero spinning in silhouette, finally emerging again into a seated swing.

Photo by Kyle Purcell.

Photo by Kyle Purcell.

HANNAH *comes on stage.* MAEV *lowers from the swing. They look at each other through the plexiglass wall, overlapping each other's images.* MAEV *exits as* HANNAH *turns around and faces the audience.*

HANNAH HERSELF: I'm Hannah. They told me I had to do the rest myself.

Beat.

When Elijah's eighteen months old, I look online to see if he's meeting his developmental goalposts. I look at language first, because . . . I'm worried about it. I read that Elijah's supposed to have a vocabulary of thirty words. So I decide to record him talking for one hour. He says a

42

hundred and nine words. In an hour. At one and a half years old he says "calculator," "complicated," and "transparent." By the time he turns two he says "horizontal," "esophagus," and "reconstituted."

Photo by Kyle Purcell.

Beat.

And listen, when I'm around other people who watch me parent I hear— through their ears—how inept I am, how much I fumble it. But when I'm alone with Elijah, I have no trouble hooking into the silly sense of humour he likes. I hear myself describe the world to him—the colour of the sky (white) the birds (black) the ocean (blue) . . .

Beat.

In those moments, the joy is . . . unreal. I didn't know I had joy like this in me. Sometimes in these moments of joy—I go outside myself and watch the film of me and Elijah and I think *nothing* can be this good. It goes down and down. It's as though I've plunged into water, and in the water is glitter.

Beat.

What I'm trying to say is . . .

Beat.

I'm a good mother.

Beat.

I'm a good mother.

Beat.

And I am the origins of the world.

Beat.

And I don't have to be sorry.

Out in the hallway, outside the theatre after the performance, is an installation, around which audience members can gather. It is a third aquarium. It's filled with baby bath toys, and in the middle of it, a paper floats. On the paper the following words are typed:

At some point during this project, Hannah was tasked with writing a (fake) biography for Elijah. Here is what she wrote:

Elijah grows up and gets a Ph.D. in physics from the University of Toronto. He works on Bay Street, setting up and administering a series of robots that can buy, sell, and trade stocks.

He meets his wife, Aqsa, on a softball team for financial advisers. Aqsa came to Canada from Syria as a refugee during the second Trudeau administration.

Elijah dies of heart failure at the age of eighty-one. In his final moments, he lies on the ground outside his summer home as one of his grandchildren dials 911. Elijah looks up at the birds (black) and the sky (white).

ACKNOWLEDGEMENTS

Our show was developed over five years with the contributions and care of many many people. We'd like to acknowledge and thank the following:

Tova Smith for her immense initial contribution to the piece.

The dozens of mothers and fathers we interviewed in our early development days, and to Darwin Lyons for assisting us.

Our families: Anthony and Sophia Black, Christian and Elijah Barry, Alan and Esmé Dilworth, Mary and Richard Beaty, Marilyn and George Kerr, Allan Moscovitch, Julie White, Joanne Farkas.

Our spectacular designers: Camellia Koo, Cameron Davis, Debashis Sinha, Leigh Ann Vardy, Kaileigh Krysztofiak, Erika Connor.

The Theatre Centre and the tremendous support provided through their residency program and in our premiere production, specifically Franco Boni, Aislinn Rose, Kyle Purcell, Alexis Eastman, and Sascha Cole, with thanks to Carrie Sager.

A special thanks to Alexis Eastman, Kyle Purcell, and Tanya Rintoul for setting up and running the child care program at the Theatre Centre that made our shows accessible to parents who needed/wanted child care to attend our shows.

The granting bodies who helped fund development and production: Arts Nova Scotia, the Canada Council for the Arts, the Ontario Arts Council, and the Toronto Arts Council.

Crow's Theatre for hosting our second production, specifically Chris Abraham and Margaret Evans, with thanks to Suzanne Cheriton.

Our Crow's production stage manager Natasha Bean-Smith and production manager Wesley McKenzie.

Catherine Hernandez and Claudia Dey, and Joanne O'Sullivan and Christy Bruce for the pre-show performances of their beautiful work.

Expect Theatre's Laura Mullin and Chris Tolley for recording the audio version of the play for the CBC Podcasts PlayME series.

Playwrights Canada Press for this publication, with thanks to Blake Sproule and Annie Gibson.

Hannah Moscovitch is an acclaimed Canadian playwright, TV writer, and librettist whose work has been widely produced in Canada and around the world. Recent stage work includes *Sexual Misconduct of the Middle Classes* and *Old Stock: A Refugee Love Story* (co-created with Christian Barry and Ben Caplan). Hannah has been the recipient of numerous awards, including the Governor General's Literary Award, the Trillium Book Award, the Nova Scotia Masterworks Arts Award, the Scotsman Fringe First and the Herald Angel Awards at the Edinburgh Festival Fringe, and the prestigious Windham-Campbell Prize administered by Yale University. She has been nominated for the international Susan Smith Blackburn Prize, the Drama Desk Award, and Canada's Siminovitch Prize in Theatre. She is a playwright-in-residence at Tarragon Theatre in Toronto. She lives in Halifax.

Maev Beaty is a critically acclaimed actor, writer, and voice-over artist, originating roles in over two dozen Canadian premieres (Hannah Moscovitch's *Bunny*, Kate Hennig's *The Last Wife*, Judith Thompson's *Palace of the End*, Sharon Pollock's *Angel's Trumpet*); co-writing and starring in award-winning theatre (*Secret Life of a Mother, Montparnasse, Dance of the Red Skirts*); interpreting classic lead roles across the country and over several seasons at the Stratford Festival (*King Lear, She Stoops to Conquer, A Midsummer Night's Dream*); and acting in epic theatre endeavours (Soulpepper's *August: Osage County*, Sheep No Wool/ Outside the March/Convergence's *Passion Play*, Nightwood's *Penelopiad*, Volcano's *Another Africa*, Theatrefront's *The Mill*). She is a Toronto Theatre Critics' Award winner and has won multiple Dora Mavor Moore Awards, having been nominated for the award fourteen times. She lives in Toronto.

Ann-Marie Kerr is an award-winning theatre director, actor, and teacher based in Halifax. Select directing credits include *Concord Floral* (Fountain School of Performing Arts, Halifax), *Secret Life of A Mother* (Theatre Centre and Crow's Theatre, Toronto), *One Discordant Violin* (2b theatre company, Halifax, and 59E59 Theatre, New York), *Bed and Breakfast* (Soulpepper Theatre Company, Toronto), *A Christmas Carol* (Theatre New Brunswick, Fredericton), *Daughter* (SummerWorks, Toronto, and Battersea Arts Centre, London), *Snake in the Grass* (Neptune Theatre, Halifax), *I, Claudia* (Globe Theatre, Regina, and Neptune Theatre, Halifax), *Stranger to Hard Work* (Eastern Front Theatre, national tour), *The Circle* (Alberta Theatre Projects, Calgary), *The Debacle* (Zuppa Theatre Company, Halifax), and *Invisible Atom* (2b theatre company, Halifax, and international tour). She is a graduate of L'École internationale de théâtre Jacques Lecoq and York University and is the former artistic associate of the Magnetic North Theatre Festival.

First edition: January 2022
Printed and bound in Canada by Rapido Books, Montreal

Jacket art and design by Julia Hutt

Photos from pages vii–xi © Dahlia Katz
Photos from pages 4–43 © Kyle Purcell
Photos of Hannah Moscovitch and Maev Beaty © Alejandro
Santiago

**PLAYWRIGHTS
CANADA PRESS**

202-269 Richmond St. W.
Toronto, ON
M5V 1X1

416.703.0013
info@playwrightscanada.com
www.playwrightscanada.com
@playcanpress